Informing the legislative debate since 1914

U.S. Circuit and District Court Nominations During President Obama's First Five Years: Comparative Analysis With Recent Presidents

Barry J. McMillion

Analyst on the Federal Judiciary

January 24, 2014

Congressional Research Service

7-5700

www.crs.gov

R43369

Summary

The selection and confirmation process for U.S. circuit and district court judges is of continuing interest to Congress. Recent Senate debates over judicial nominations have focused on issues such as the relative degree of success of President Barack Obama's nominees in gaining Senate confirmation compared with other recent Presidents, as well as the relative prevalence of vacant judgeships compared to years past, and the effect of delayed judicial appointments on judicial vacancy levels. This report addresses these issues, and others, by providing a statistical analysis of nominations to U.S. circuit and district court judgeships during the first five years of President Obama's time in office and that of his three most recent two-term predecessors. Some of the report's findings include the following:

- During his first five years in office, President Obama nominated 57 persons to U.S. circuit court judgeships. Of the 57, 41 (71.9%) were also confirmed during this same five-year period. The 41 confirmed Obama circuit court nominees represented the second-lowest number of nominees confirmed during recent Presidents' first five years. President Clinton had the lowest number at 37. The percentage of circuit court nominees confirmed during President Obama's first five years, 71.9%, was also the second-lowest, while the percentage confirmed during President Clinton's, 69.8%, was the lowest. Of the four Presidents, President Reagan had both the greatest number (55) and percentage (94.8%) of circuit court nominees confirmed within the first five years of his presidency.

- Of the 226 persons nominated by President Obama to U.S. district court judgeships during his first five years, 173 (76.5%) were confirmed. Of the four Presidents, this was the lowest number and percentage of district court nominees confirmed. Of the comparison group, President Clinton had the greatest number of district court nominees confirmed during his first five years (198) while President Reagan had the greatest percentage of district court nominees confirmed (95.5%)—followed closely by the percentage of district court nominees confirmed during the first five years of the G.W. Bush presidency (93.8%).

- The average number of days elapsed from nomination to confirmation for circuit court nominees confirmed during a President's first five years ranged from 56.8 days during the Reagan presidency to 402.0 days during the G.W. Bush presidency. The median number of days from nomination to confirmation for circuit court nominees confirmed during a President's first five years ranged from 37.0 days (Reagan) to 245.0 (G.W. Bush). The average and median number of days from nomination to confirmation for President Obama's circuit nominees were 253.7 and 228.0 days, respectively.

- The average number of days elapsed from nomination to confirmation for district court nominees confirmed during a President's first five years ranged from 50.0 days during the Reagan presidency to 223.3 days during the Obama presidency. The median number of days from nomination to confirmation for district court nominees confirmed during a President's first five years ranged from 31.0 days (Reagan) to 214.0 (Obama).

- President Obama is the only President of the four for whom, during his first five years in office, a majority of U.S. circuit and district court nominees waited more than 180 days to be confirmed after being nominated.

- President Obama is the only President of the four for whom there was an increase in the percentage of both U.S. circuit and district court judgeships that were vacant from January 1 of his fifth year in office to January 1 of his sixth year.

- The percentage of circuit court vacancies deemed "judicial emergencies" increased from January 1 of the fifth year to January 1 of the sixth year of the Obama presidency and decreased over the same period during the Clinton and G.W. Bush presidencies. The percentage of district court vacancies deemed judicial emergencies increased from January 1 of the fifth to the sixth years of the Clinton and Obama presidencies and decreased over the same period during the G.W. Bush presidency.

Contents

Figures

Tables

Contacts

Introduction

Article III, Section I, of the Constitution provides, in part, that the "judicial Power of the United States, shall be vested in one supreme Court, and in such inferior Courts as the Congress may from time to time ordain and establish." It further provides that Justices on the Supreme Court and judges on lower courts established by Congress under Article III have what effectively has come to mean life tenure, holding office "during good Behaviour."[1] Along with the Supreme Court, the courts that constitute the Article III courts in the federal system are the U.S. circuit courts of appeals, the U.S. district courts, and the U.S. Court of International Trade.[2]

This report concerns nominations made by President Obama and other recent Presidents to the U.S. circuit courts of appeals and the U.S. district courts.[3] Outside the report's scope are the occasional nominations that these Presidents made to the Supreme Court and the U.S. Court of International Trade.[4]

In recent Congresses, there has been ongoing interest in the process by which U.S. circuit and district court judges are nominated by the President and approved by the Senate. During Senate debates over judicial nominations, differing perspectives have been expressed about the relative degree of success of a President's nominees in gaining Senate confirmation, compared with the nominees of other recent Presidents.[5] Additionally, Senate debate often has concerned whether a President's judicial nominees, relative to the nominees of other recent Presidents, had to wait longer before receiving consideration by the Senate Judiciary Committee or "up-or-down" floor votes on confirmation.[6] Of related concern to Congress has been increases in recent years in the number of vacant judgeships in the federal judiciary, the frequency with which vacant judgeships

---

[1] Pursuant to this constitutional language, Article III judges may hold office for as long as they live or until they voluntarily leave office. A President has no power to remove them from office. Article III judges, however, may be removed by Congress through the process of impeachment by the House and conviction by the Senate.

[2] The U.S. Court of International Trade is a nine-member court with nationwide jurisdiction over civil actions arising out of the customs and international trade laws of the United States.

[3] The U.S. courts of appeals take appeals from federal district court decisions and are also empowered to review the decisions of many administrative agencies. Altogether, 179 appellate court judgeships for 13 courts of appeals are currently authorized by law. In this report, nominations to U.S. courts of appeals judgeships are frequently referred to as "circuit court nominations." U.S. district courts are the federal trial courts of general jurisdiction. Altogether, 673 Article III U.S. district court judgeships are currently authorized by law. For further background information on U.S. courts of appeals and district courts, see CRS Report R43058, *President Obama's First-Term U.S. Circuit and District Court Nominations: An Analysis and Comparison with Presidents Since Reagan*, by Barry J. McMillion.

[4] The scope of this report also does not include the relatively rare nominations made by a President to territorial district court judgeships, which were established by Congress pursuant to its authority to govern the territories under Article IV of the Constitution. The three U.S. territorial courts are located in Guam, the Northern Mariana Islands, and the U.S. Virgin Islands. Judges confirmed to these courts serve 10-year terms (rather than "during good Behaviour"). Like Article III courts, territorial courts hear cases arising out of federal law, their decisions may be appealed to a U.S. circuit court of appeals, and their judicial nominations are referred to the Senate Judiciary Committee.

[5] See, for example, Sen. Patrick J. Leahy, "Executive Session," Remarks in the Senate, *Congressional Record*, daily edition, August 1, 2013, pp. S6147-S6148. See also Sen. Chuck Grassley, "Executive Session," Remarks in the Senate, *Congressional Record*, daily edition, September 9, 2013, p. S6285.

[6] Senate debate on these issues also occurred during President Obama's first term. See, for example, contrasting views on these and related issues in floor remarks by Senators Leahy and Grassley in "Executive Session," Remarks in the Senate, *Congressional Record*, daily edition, May 7, 2012, pp. S2907-2908 (Leahy) and pp. S2909-2910 (Grassley); and in "Nomination of George Levi Russell III, To Be United States District Judge for the District of Maryland," Remarks in the Senate, *Congressional Record*, daily edition, May 14, 2012, pp. S3117-3119 (Leahy) and pp. S3120-3121 (Grassley).

are considered "judicial emergencies," and the effect of delays in the processing of judicial nominations on filling vacancies.[7]

Perhaps in response to some of the issues described above, the Senate, on November 21, 2013,

> reinterpreted the application of Senate Rule XXII to floor consideration of presidential nominations by overturning a ruling of the chair on appeal. For nominations other than to the Supreme Court, the new precedent lowered the vote threshold by which cloture can be invoked—from three-fifths of the Senate to a simple majority of those voting, thereby enabling a supportive majority to reach an 'up-or-down' vote on confirming a nomination. Reaching a confirmation vote, however, still requires either unanimous consent or a successful cloture process, ...[8]

In light of continued Senate interest in the judicial selection and confirmation process, this report seeks to inform the ongoing debate in four ways: (1) by using various statistical measures to compare the progress of President Obama's judicial nominees, during his first five years, in advancing through the Senate confirmation process with that of the judicial nominees during the first five years of the three most recent preceding Presidents who served two terms (Ronald Reagan, George W. Bush, and Bill Clinton); (2) by providing statistics related to the length of time it has taken President Obama and his three predecessors to nominate individuals to vacant circuit and district court judgeships; and (3) by providing statistics related to judicial vacancies existing at the beginning of each President's fifth and sixth years in office.[9]

For the purposes of this report, a President's first five years in office are defined as the period of time between January 20, the date he assumed office during the first calendar year of his presidency, to December 31 of his fifth calendar year in office (rather than to January 19, which falls during his sixth calendar year in office). Operationalizing a President's fifth year in this manner allows for the analysis to coincide more closely with dates for which congressional action on judicial nominations might occur (prior to the Senate adjourning *sine die*).[10]

---

[7] See, for example, Sen. Patrick J. Leahy, "Judicial Nominations in 2013," Remarks in the Senate, *Congressional Record*, daily edition, December 20, 2013, p. S9092. Concern over judicial vacancies has also been expressed by Chief Justice John G. Roberts, Jr., and by his predecessor, Chief Justice William Rehnquist. Chief Justice Roberts, noting that vacancies are not evenly distributed across judicial districts, has stated that "a persistent problem has developed in the process of filling judicial vacancies.... This has created acute difficulties for some judicial districts. Sitting judges in those districts have been burdened with extraordinary caseloads." Chief Justice John G. Roberts, Jr., "2010 Year-End Report on the Federal Judiciary," Jan. 2011, http://www.supremecourt.gov/publicinfo/year-end/2010year-endreport.pdf. Similarly, former Chief Justice Rehnquist argued that "[j]udicial vacancies can contribute to a backlog of cases, undue delays in civil cases, and stopgap measures to shift judicial personnel where they are most needed. Vacancies cannot remain at such high levels indefinitely without eroding the quality of justice that traditionally has been associated with the federal judiciary." Chief Justice William Rehnquist, "1997 Year-End Report on the Federal Judiciary," Third Branch, Jan. 1998.

[8] CRS Report R43331, *Majority Cloture for Nominations: Implications and the "Nuclear" Proceedings*, by Valerie Heitshusen.

[9] For a discussion of the various factors which might help explain differences or variations found in judicial nominations statistics and judicial vacancies across presidencies, see CRS Report R43058, *President Obama's First-Term U.S. Circuit and District Court Nominations: An Analysis and Comparison with Presidents Since Reagan*, by Barry J. McMillion.

[10] An adjournment *sine die* is an adjournment that terminates an annual session of Congress.

Number and Percentage of Confirmed Judicial Nominees

This section of the report contains various statistical measures to compare the judicial nomination and confirmation process during the first five years of the Obama presidency to the presidencies of his three immediate two-term predecessors (Presidents Reagan, G.W. Bush, and Clinton).[11] It first compares the number and percentage of U.S. circuit and district court nominees who were confirmed during the first five years of the Reagan, Clinton, G.W. Bush, and Obama presidencies. It then provides, for the same four Presidents, a comparison of selected features of the judicial nomination and confirmation process during each President's first five years in office. The section concludes by comparing the percentage of circuit and district court judgeships vacant at the beginning of each President's fifth and sixth years in office as well as the percentage of such vacancies considered "judicial emergencies."

This report does not analyze or take a position on the number or percentage of a President's judicial nominees that would be appropriate for the Senate to confirm or on the average (or median) length of time that would be appropriate for, or needed by, the Senate Judiciary Committee to process judicial nominations or for the Senate to take final action on them.[12] Similarly, this report does not analyze or take a position on the appropriate amount of time for an Administration to select nominees for circuit and district court judgeships.

U.S. Circuit Court Nominees

Table 1 presents, during the first five years of a presidency for Presidents Reagan through Obama, the total number of circuit court nominees, the total number (and percentage) of circuit nominees confirmed by the end of a President's fifth year in office,[13] the number (and percentage) confirmed after his fifth year, and the number (and percentage) of circuit nominees never confirmed.[14] While Presidents sometimes have nominated particular individuals to a court more

---

[11] Most of the statistics presented and discussed in this report were generated from an internal CRS judicial nominations database. Other data sources, however, are noted where appropriate. As mentioned above, the statistics account only for nominations made to U.S. circuit court and district court judgeships.

[12] The "average" or "mean" is the arithmetic mean (both terms are used interchangeably throughout this report), while the "median" indicates the middle value for a particular set of numbers.

[13] Not included as a confirmed nominee is any individual who received a recess appointment by the President and who was not subsequently confirmed by the Senate during that same President's first five years in office. So, for example, Charles W. Pickering, Sr., received a recess appointment by President G.W. Bush to the U.S. Court of Appeals for the Fifth Circuit on January 16, 2004. Mr. Pickering was not ultimately confirmed by the Senate and his judicial service ended on December 8, 2004. Consequently, he is not included as a confirmed circuit court nominee during the G.W. Bush presidency. For a discussion of recess appointments, generally, see CRS Report RS21308, *Recess Appointments: Frequently Asked Questions*, by Henry B. Hogue.

[14] A judicial nomination may fail to receive Senate confirmation because (1) the full Senate votes against the nomination; (2) the President withdraws the nomination, either because the Senate Judiciary Committee (i) has voted against reporting it favorably, (ii) has made clear its intention not to act on the nomination, or (iii) because the nomination, even if reported, is likely to fact substantial opposition on the Senate floor; (3) the nominee himself or herself has requested that the nomination be withdrawn; or (4) the Senate, without confirming or rejecting the nomination, returns the nomination to the President under Rule XXXI, paragraph 6 of the *Standing Rules of the Senate* after it has adjourned or been in recess for more than 30 days and the President does not subsequently resubmit the nomination to the Senate.

than once, **Table 1** counts such nominees only once (as does **Table 2** below). In other words, neither table accounts for multiple nominations of the same individual to the same court.

Table 1 reveals that each President nominated between 50 and 60 individuals to circuit court judgeships during his first five years, with Presidents Reagan and Obama nominating the greatest number of individuals (58 and 57, respectively). For President Reagan, all but three of the circuit court nominees who were nominated during his first five years in office were also confirmed by the end of his fifth year. President Clinton had the lowest percentage of circuit court nominees confirmed by the end of his fifth year in office (69.8%), followed by Presidents Obama (71.9%) and G.W. Bush (77.8%).

Ten circuit court nominees who were nominated during President Clinton's first five years were eventually confirmed later in his presidency (i.e., during the sixth year or later), raising the overall confirmation percentage of individuals *nominated to circuit courts during the first five years of his presidency* to 88.7%. This compares to a high of 96.6% for individuals nominated during President Reagan's first five years and a low of 81.5% for those nominated during President G.W. Bush's first five years.

Of those individuals nominated during the first five years of a presidency, President G.W. Bush had the highest percentage who were never confirmed (18.5%), followed by Presidents Clinton (11.3%) and Reagan (3.4%).

Table 1. U.S. Circuit Court Nominees: Number Nominated, Number Confirmed, Percentage Confirmed During First Five Years

| President | Number Nominated By End of 5th Year | Number (Percent) Confirmed | | Overall Number (Percent) Confirmed of All Those Nominated By End of 5th Year | Number (Percent) Never Confirmed |
		By End of 5th Year	After 5th Year		
Reagan	58	55 (94.8)	1 (1.7)	56 (96.6)	2 (3.4)
Clinton	53	37 (69.8)	10 (18.9)	47 (88.7)	6 (11.3)
G.W. Bush	54	42 (77.8)	2 (3.7)	44 (81.5)	10 (18.5)
Obama	57	41 (71.9)	TBD	TBD	TBD

Source: Internal CRS judicial nominations database.

Notes: This table shows the total number of individuals nominated for circuit court judgeships during a President's first five years in office as well as the number and percentage of nominees confirmed during his first five years and after his fifth year. The table also shows the number and percentage of circuit court nominees who were nominated during a President's first five years who were never confirmed by the Senate. "TBD" is "to be determined" over the remaining years of the Obama presidency. As of the writing of this report, President Obama has had one circuit court nominee confirmed in January of his sixth calendar year in office (Robert L. Wilkins was confirmed by the Senate on January 13, 2014).

U.S. District Court Nominees

Table 2 presents, during the first five years of the Reagan, Clinton, G.W. Bush, and Obama presidencies, the total number of district court nominees, the total number (and percentage) of district nominees confirmed by the end of each President's fifth year in office, the number (and percentage) confirmed after his fifth year, and the number (and percentage) of district court nominees never confirmed.

The table reveals that each President nominated between 194 and 239 individuals to district court judgeships during his first five years in office, with Presidents Clinton and Obama nominating the greatest number of individuals (239 and 226, respectively). Presidents Clinton and Obama, however, also had the lowest percentages of those individuals confirmed during their first five years (82.8% and 76.5%, respectively). President Reagan had the greatest percentage of individuals who were nominated during his first five years also confirmed prior to the end of his fifth year in office (95.5%), followed by President G.W. Bush (93.8%).

Twenty-two district court nominees who were nominated during President Clinton's first five years in office were eventually confirmed later in his presidency (i.e., during his sixth year or later), raising the overall confirmation percentage of individuals nominated during the first five years of his presidency to 92.0%. This compares to an overall confirmation rate of 99.0% for individuals nominated during President G.W. Bush's first five years and 98.5% of those nominated during President Reagan's first five years.

Table 2. U.S. District Court Nominees: Number Nominated, Number Confirmed, Percentage Confirmed During First Five Years

President	Number Nominated By End of 5th Year	Number (Percent) Confirmed		Overall Number (Percent) Confirmed of All Those Nominated By End of 5th Year	Number (Percent) Never Confirmed
		By End of 5th Year	After 5th Year		
Reagan	200	191 (95.5)	6 (3.0)	197 (98.5)	3 (1.5)
Clinton	239	198 (82.8)	22 (9.2)	220 (92.0)	19 (7.9)
G.W. Bush	194	182 (93.8)	10 (5.2)	192 (99.0)	2 (1.0)
Obama	226	173 (76.5)	TBD	TBD	TBD

Source: Internal CRS judicial nominations database.

Notes: This table shows the total number of individuals nominated for district court judgeships during a President's first five years in office as well as the number and percentage of nominees confirmed during his first five years and after his fifth year. The table also shows the number and percentage of district court nominees who were nominated during a President's first five years who were never confirmed by the Senate. "TBD" is "to be determined" over the remaining years of the Obama presidency.

Of those individuals nominated during the first five years of a presidency, President Clinton had the highest percentage of nominees who were never confirmed (7.9%), followed by Presidents Reagan (1.5%) and G.W. Bush (1.0%).

Confirmation of Judicial Nominees During a President's Fifth Year

There is variation across the four Presidents in the number of U.S. circuit and district court nominees confirmed solely during a President's fifth year in office. The number of circuit court nominees confirmed during a fifth year ranged from a high of 22 during the Reagan presidency to a low of 7 during both the Clinton and G.W. Bush presidencies. President Obama had 11 circuit court nominees confirmed during his fifth year in office.[15]

For district court nominees, the number of nominees confirmed during a fifth year ranged from a high of 62 during the Reagan presidency to a low of 14 during the G.W. Bush presidency. For Presidents Clinton and Obama, 29 and 32 district court nominees were confirmed, respectively, during their fifth years in office.[16]

Although President Obama had the second greatest number of district court nominees confirmed by the Senate during his fifth year in office, he trailed (as shown in **Table 2**) the other three Presidents in both the overall number and percentage of district court nominees confirmed during the first five years. This might reflect, in part, the relatively longer time it has taken the Senate to confirm President Obama's district court nominees.[17]

Judicial Nominations Still Awaiting Senate Action At End of Fifth Year

Some judicial nominations at the end of a President's fifth year in office might still be awaiting action by the Judiciary Committee or the full Senate when the Senate adjourns *sine die*.[18] For the purposes of this report, nominations awaiting Judiciary Committee action include those for which a hearing had not yet been held as well as those for which a hearing had been held but not reported by the committee.[19] Nominations awaiting action by the full Senate are those that, due to being reported by the Judiciary Committee, are pending on the *Executive Calendar*.

President Obama, compared to the other three Presidents, had at the end of his fifth year in office the second greatest number of circuit court nominees whose nominations were still awaiting action by either the Judiciary Committee or full Senate. Altogether there were 10 circuit court nominees with nominations still awaiting committee or floor action by the end of December 2013.[20] These 10 nominees accounted for 17.5% of the 57 individuals nominated to circuit courts

---

[15] The 22 circuit court nominees confirmed during President Reagan's fifth year in office accounted for 40.0% of the 55 circuit court nominees confirmed during his first five years in office. For Presidents Clinton, G.W. Bush, and Obama, the number of circuit court nominees confirmed during each President's first five years accounted for 18.9%, 16.7%, and 26.8%, respectively, of the total number of circuit court nominees confirmed during his first five years.

[16] The 62 district court nominees confirmed during President Reagan's fifth year in office accounted for 32.5% of the 191 district court nominees confirmed during his first five years in office. For Presidents Clinton, G.W. Bush, and Obama, the number of district court nominees confirmed during each President's first five years accounted for 14.6%, 7.7%, and 18.5%, respectively, of the total number of district court nominees confirmed during his first five years.

[17] **Figure 2**, which appears later in this report, addresses this point further.

[18] As mentioned above, adjournment *sine die* is an adjournment that terminates an annual session of Congress.

[19] The committee is not required to meet and consider reporting a nomination after a hearing has been held, but once such a meeting has been scheduled, any committee member may delay action on the nomination under committee rules. Specifically, Judiciary Committee rules state that "[a]t the request of any member, or by action of the Chairman, ... [a] nomination on the agenda of the Committee may be held over until the next meeting of the Committee or for one week, whichever occurs later." 157 Cong. Rec. S837 (daily ed. Feb. 17, 2011). Consequently, any committee member can delay the vote on reporting a nomination for one week, or longer (e.g., when a recess or adjournment occurs).

[20] Not all of these nominations were "late" nominations, which are, for the purposes of this report, considered nominations submitted to the Senate during the last quarter of the calendar year (after October 1). Of the ten nominations, seven had been received in the Senate prior to October 1, 2013. Nine of the ten nominations were returned to the President on January 3, 2014 (all were subsequently resubmitted to the Senate on January 6, 2014). Robert L. Wilkins's nomination to the D.C. Circuit Court of Appeals was not returned to the President at the end of the first (continued...)

---

by President Obama by the end of his fifth year. At the end of the fifth years of the Clinton and G.W. Bush presidencies there were 13 and 7 nominees, respectively, awaiting action. These nominees accounted for 24.5% and 13.0%, respectively, of individuals nominated during the first five years of the Clinton and G.W. Bush presidencies. By the end of President Reagan's fifth year in office there was one circuit court nomination still awaiting action (accounting for 1.7% of those nominated during his first five years).

President Obama had the greatest number of district court nominees pending before either the Judiciary Committee or the full Senate by the end of his fifth year in office compared to his three predecessors. By the end of December 2013, there were 46 district court nominees with nominations awaiting committee action or final Senate action (accounting for 20.4% of all those nominated to district court judgeships during President Obama's first five years).[21] In contrast, 11 district court nominees were awaiting committee or final Senate action by the end of President G.W. Bush's fifth year in office (accounting for 5.7% of those nominated during his first five years), while 30 district court nominees were awaiting committee or floor action by the end of President Clinton's fifth year in office (accounting for 12.6% of those nominated to district court judgeships during his first five years). At the end of President Reagan's fifth year in office, eight district court nominees were still awaiting action by the Judiciary Committee or full Senate (accounting for 4.0% of his nominees).

Selected Features of the Nomination and Confirmation Process

Like other parts of this report, the discussion under this heading is based upon nomination and confirmation statistics from each President's first five years in office. For the discussion related specifically to the confirmation process in the Senate, the statistics generally account only for those nominees who were confirmed by the Senate during a President's first five years (thus excluding from the analysis nominees who were never confirmed or who were later confirmed in a President's term, i.e., during his sixth year or later, and, for President Obama, those nominations for which final disposition cannot yet be discerned).

Length of Time from Vacancy to Nomination

Figure 1 tracks by President, from Reagan to Obama, the average and median number of days from a judicial vacancy occurring to a President nominating someone for that vacancy.[22] Included in the calculations are individuals, whether confirmed or not, who were nominated to circuit and district court judgeships during a President's first five years.[23] If a nomination was for a vacancy

---

(...continued)

session of the 113th Congress, and he was confirmed by the Senate on January 13, 2014.

[21] Of the 46 nominations, 35 had been received in the Senate prior to October 1, 2013 (including 23 nominations submitted prior to the August recess). The 46 nominations were returned to the President on January 3, 2014 (45 of the nominations, as of January 13, 2014, had been resubmitted).

[22] The statistics reported for **Figure 1** are based on CRS analysis of data provided by the Administrative Office of U.S. Courts and the Legislative Information System (LIS) of the U.S. Congress.

[23] A President will occasionally nominate someone after an active, full-time judge has announced his or her intent to retire or take senior status on a specified future date but before the vacancy actually occurs. These relatively rare (continued...)

---

existing prior to a President taking office, the date the President first took office (January 20 of his first year) was used as the date a vacancy occurred for the purpose of calculating the days elapsed from vacancy to nomination. If a nomination was made for a vacancy occurring while a President was in office, the actual date of the vacancy occurring was used in the calculations.[24]

U.S. Circuit Court Vacancies

It took President Clinton, on average, the longest amount of time to nominate individuals to circuit court vacancies (370.6 days). Presidents Obama and G.W. Bush took, on average, 261.6 and 256.4 days, respectively, while President Reagan took 234.3 days.

In terms of the median number of days from vacancy to nomination, both Presidents G.W. Bush and Obama took less than 200 days to nominate individuals to circuit court vacancies (146 and 162.5 days, respectively). President Reagan took 234 days while President Clinton took 372 days.

U.S. District Court Vacancies

As for district court nominees, President Obama took, on average, the longest amount of time to nominate individuals to district court vacancies (348.3 days), while President G.W. Bush took the least amount of time (258.8 days). President Reagan took, on average, 258.8 days, while President Clinton took 341.6 days.

In terms of the median number of days from vacancy to nomination, it took President Clinton the longest amount of time to nominate individuals to district court vacancies (303 days), while President G.W. Bush took the least amount of time (194 days). President Reagan took 240 days and President Obama took 288.5 days.

It is not clear based on these statistics alone whether there is a relationship between the length of time it takes a President to nominate individuals to vacant judgeships and the number or percentage of those individuals confirmed by the Senate. President Clinton, for example, took nearly as long as President Obama, on average, to nominate individuals to vacant district court judgeships. Despite this, there were 25 more district court judges confirmed during the first five years of the Clinton presidency than during the first five years of the Obama presidency.

(...continued)

instances of an individual being nominated by a President *prior to* a judicial vacancy formally occurring are not included in the analysis.

[24] In cases when a nomination was unsuccessful (e.g., a nomination is withdrawn by the President or returned by the Senate to the President and not resubmitted) and a President nominates a different individual to the same judgeship as the unsuccessful nominee, the vacancy date (or "appointment opportunity date") is calculated as the date the preceding unsuccessful nomination was withdrawn or returned.

Figure 1. U.S. Circuit Court Vacancies: Mean and Median Number of Days from Vacancy to Nomination for Individuals Nominated During First Five Years

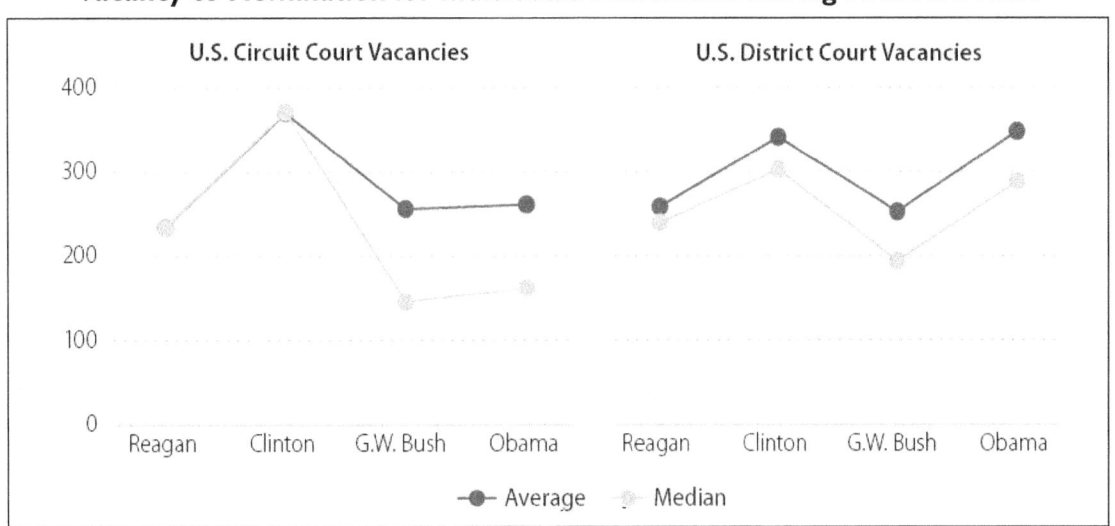

Source: Internal CRS judicial vacancies database.

Notes: This figure shows the mean and median number of days from a judicial vacancy occurring to a President nominating an individual to that vacancy.

For his part, the speed with which the President submits judicial nominations to the Senate reflects factors both within an Administration's control and outside its control. Factors within an Administration's control include the priority a particular President places on filling judicial vacancies, the number of individuals in the White House involved in identifying and screening potential nominees, and the nature of the vetting process to which the nominee is subject prior to his or her nomination being submitted to the Senate.

Factors outside an Administration's control include whether a vacancy on the Supreme Court occurs (thus perhaps delaying a President's selection of lower court nominees)[25] and whether (or how quickly) Senators submit to the President their recommendations for a vacancy existing in their particular state.[26]

---

[25] In 1993, for example, President Bill Clinton did not send his first district court nominations to the Senate until August 6. Likely delaying the President's initial selection of lower court nominations in 1993 was the March 19, 1993, announcement by Justice Byron R. White of his intention to retire from the Supreme Court when it adjourned for the summer. President Clinton engaged in a three-month selection search for Justice White's successor, announcing on June 14, 1993, his selection of Ruth Bader Ginsburg as his Supreme Court nominee. For the President, selecting and nominating a person to fill a vacancy on the Supreme Court evidently took priority over providing the Senate with nominations to lower court judgeships. The Ginsburg nomination, in turn, was a primary object of attention for the Senate Judiciary Committee during June and July 1993, and subsequently as well for the Senate, which voted to confirm Justice Ginsburg on August 3, 1993, four days before the start of its August recess. As it had with the President, the Ginsburg nomination, for the Judiciary Committee and the Senate as a whole, presumably would have taken priority over lower court nominations had any been received prior to the Supreme Court nomination.

[26] Home state Senators traditionally play an important role in the selection of district and, to a lesser extent, circuit court judges. The pace might be slowed by communication between the President and those Senators who represent states with vacant federal judgeships. Additionally, if the home state Senators are themselves slow in recommending a candidate, or if they and the President cannot agree on a suitable candidate, the nomination of an individual to fill a vacant judgeship may be delayed. For more information on the role of home state Senators, see CRS Report RL34405, *Role of Home State Senators in the Selection of Lower Federal Court Judges*, by Barry J. McMillion and Denis Steven Rutkus.

Length of Time from Nomination to Confirmation

Figure 2 tracks by President the average and median number of days from nomination to confirmation for all circuit and district court nominees confirmed during a President's first five years in office.[27] If a nominee was nominated more than once by a President during his first five years (and he or she was also confirmed within those five years), the first date he or she was nominated was used to calculate the days elapsed from nomination to confirmation.

U.S. Circuit Court Nominees

President G.W. Bush's circuit court nominees who were confirmed during his first five years waited, on average, the longest period of time from first nomination to confirmation (402 days). President Obama's nominees waited, on average, the second-longest period of time (253.7 days), followed by the circuit court nominees of Presidents Clinton (158.2 days) and Reagan (56.8 days).

In terms of the median number of days from nomination to confirmation, President G.W. Bush's circuit court nominees also waited the longest period of time from nomination to confirmation (245 days), followed by President Obama's circuit nominees (228 days). The circuit court nominees who were confirmed during President Clinton's first five years had a median wait time of 108 days while President Reagan's circuit nominees had a median wait time of 37 days.

Figure 2. U.S. Circuit and District Court Nominees: Mean and Median Number of Days from Nomination to Confirmation for Nominees Confirmed During First Five Years

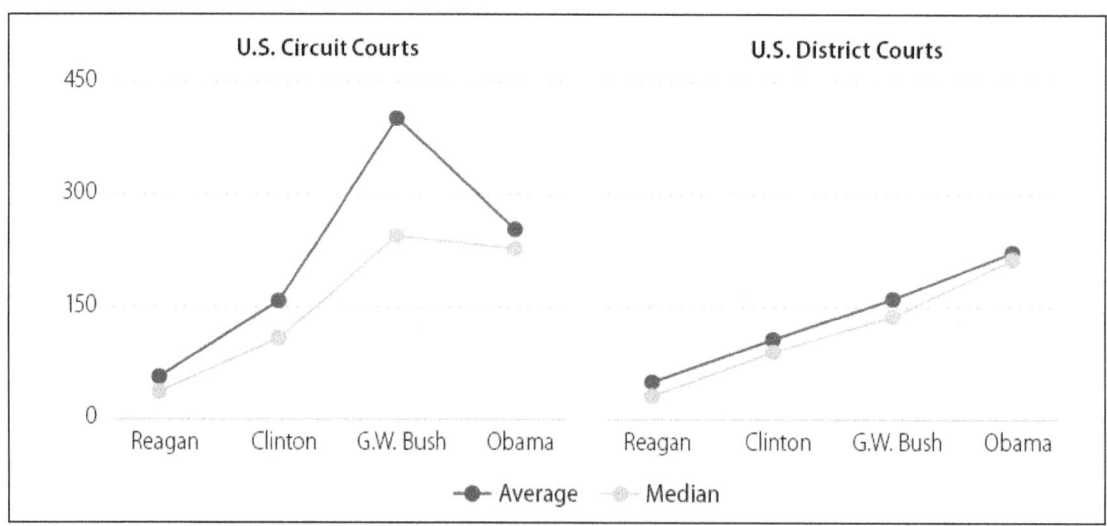

Source: Internal CRS judicial nominations database.

---

[27] As mentioned above, the "average" or "mean" is the arithmetic mean (both terms are used interchangeably throughout this report), while the "median" indicates the middle value for a particular set of numbers. In this case, the median is the middle value for the number of days from nomination to confirmation for a particular President's circuit or district court nominees. Although the average (also referred to as the mean) is the more commonly used measure, the median is less affected by outliers or extreme cases, e.g., nominees whose elapsed time from first nomination to confirmation was unusually long or short. Consequently, the median might be a better measure of central tendency.

Notes: This figure shows the mean and median number of days from first nomination to confirmation for all U.S. circuit and district court nominees who were confirmed during a President's first five years in office.

An additional way to analyze the data concerning the length of time from nomination to confirmation is to calculate the percentage of judicial nominees for whom, once nominated, it takes a certain length of time to be confirmed.[28] For example, as **Table 3** shows, a majority (61.8%) of President Reagan's circuit court nominees were confirmed within 60 days (or approximately within two months) after first being nominated. A plurality (48.6%) of President Clinton's circuit nominees were confirmed within 61 to 120 days (or between two and four months) of first being nominated.

For President G.W. Bush's circuit court nominees, 69.0% were confirmed after more than 180 days (or six months) had elapsed after their first nomination, whereas 80.5% of President Obama's circuit nominees were confirmed after more than 180 days of first being nominated. These percentages, when compared with the average and median number of days from nomination to confirmation for President Obama's and President G.W. Bush's circuit court nominees, indicate that a greater number and percentage of President Obama's circuit court nominees who were confirmed during his first five years waited more than 6 months after being nominated. At the same time, a subset of President G.W. Bush's circuit court nominees who waited more than six months to be confirmed waited much longer than six months to be confirmed (thus, increasing the overall average wait time from nomination to confirmation during his presidency).[29]

Table 3. U.S. Circuit Court Nominees: Percentage of Nominees Confirmed Within Specified Amount of Time of First Nomination

| President | Percent of U.S. Circuit Court Nominees Confirmed by Senate | | | |
	0-60 Days	61-120 Days	121-180 Days	More than 180 Days
Reagan	61.8	29.1	3.6	5.5
Clinton	10.8	48.6	16.2	24.3
G.W. Bush	0.0	16.7	14.3	69.0
Obama	0.0	4.9	14.6	80.5

Source: Internal CRS judicial nominations database.

---

[28] Such calculations can also be done for each of the major stages of the confirmation process (i.e., from nomination to committee hearing as well as from committee report to confirmation) but are not reported in subsequent sections of this report because the primary interest of congressional clients has been the overall length of time from nomination to confirmation. The calculations, however, for each stage of the confirmation process are available upon request from the author.

[29] For example, circuit court nominees of President G.W. Bush waiting considerably longer than six months included twelve nominees who waited more than 500 days from nomination to confirmation. These nominees were Janice R. Brown, Deborah L. Cook, Richard A. Griffin, Michael W. McConnell, David W. McKeague, Susan B. Neilson, Priscilla R. Owen, William H. Pryor, Jr., John G. Roberts, Jr., Dennis W. Shedd, Jeffrey S. Sutton, and Timothy M. Tymkovich. Some of these nominations were, at the time, considered controversial (if measured by the number of "nay" votes received at the time of confirmation). Of these 12 nominees, 6 received more than 40 nay votes when confirmed by the Senate.

Notes: This table shows, for U.S. circuit court nominees confirmed during a President's first five years in office, the percentage of nominees who were confirmed by the Senate within a specified amount of time of their first nomination by the President.

U.S. District Court Nominees

As discussed above, it took President Obama longer, on average during his first five years, to nominate individuals to district court vacancies than it did the other three Presidents (see **Figure 1** above). Once nominated, however, these individuals also waited relatively longer periods of time to be confirmed compared to the district court nominees of other Presidents.

Figure 2 shows that President Obama's confirmed nominees waited, on average, 223.3 days from nomination to confirmation. President G.W. Bush's district court nominees waited, on average, 161.2 days. The district court nominees confirmed during President Clinton's first five years waited an average of 106.9 days while those confirmed during President Reagan's first five years waited 50.0 days.

The median waiting times from nomination to confirmation for district court nominees ranged from a high of 214.0 days during President Obama's first five years to a low of 31.0 days during President Reagan's first five years. For Presidents Clinton and G.W. Bush, the median waiting times from nomination to confirmation for district nominees were 90.0 and 137.5 days, respectively.

Overall, as displayed by **Table 4**, a relatively large majority (81.2%) of President Reagan's district court nominees were confirmed within 60 days (or within two months) of first being nominated. A plurality of both President Clinton's district court nominees (44.4%) and President G.W. Bush's nominees (37.3%) were confirmed between 61 and 120 days (or between two and four months) after being nominated. For President Obama's district court nominees, a majority (68.8%) waited more than 180 days (or more than six months) to be confirmed after being nominated.

Table 4. U.S. District Court Nominees: Percentage of Nominees Confirmed Within Specified Amount of Time of First Nomination

President	Percent of U.S. District Court Nominees Confirmed by Senate			
	0-60 Days	61-120 Days	121-180 Days	More than 180 Days
Reagan	81.2	11.0	2.1	5.8
Clinton	29.8	44.4	14.6	11.1
G.W. Bush	1.6	37.3	33.5	27.5
Obama	0.6	4.0	26.6	68.8

Source: Internal CRS judicial nominations database.

Notes: This table shows, for U.S. district court nominees confirmed during a President's first five years in office, the percentage of nominees who were confirmed by the Senate within a specified amount of time of their first nomination by the President.

President Obama is the only President of the four for whom, during his first five years in office, a majority of U.S. circuit and district court nominees waited more than six months (approximately 180 days) to be confirmed after being nominated.[30]

Length of Time from Nomination to Committee Hearing

Figure 3 tracks, for each of the four Presidents, the mean and median number of days from first nomination to first committee hearing for all circuit and district court nominees who received hearings during a President's first five years. All nominees who received hearings were included in the calculations, regardless of whether they were eventually confirmed or their nomination was returned, withdrawn, or rejected by the Senate.[31]

U.S. Circuit Court Nominees

Figure 3 shows that circuit court nominees of President G.W. Bush waited more days (during his first five years) to receive a hearing than did the nominees of the other four Presidents.[32] The mean and median number of days for a circuit court nominee to receive a committee hearing after being nominated ranged from a low of 28.8 and 18.5 days, respectively, during the Reagan presidency to 296.6 and 176.0 days, respectively, for the G.W. Bush presidency. President Clinton's circuit court nominees waited an average of 88.9 days to receive hearings (although the median waiting time was slightly lower—84.0 days).

Although a relatively low number and percentage of President Obama's circuit court nominees were confirmed in his first five years, his circuit court nominees received hearings relatively quickly. His circuit court nominees waited, on average, less time from first nomination to first hearing, 76.4 days, than the circuit nominees of Presidents Clinton, and G.W. Bush. Only

---

[30] For a discussion of policy options that the Senate might consider to shorten the confirmation process for lower federal court nominees, see CRS Report R43316, *Length of Time from Nomination to Confirmation for U.S. Circuit and District Court Nominees: Overview and Policy Options to Shorten the Process*, by Barry J. McMillion.

[31] In cases where a nominee received a hearing only after being renominated, the waiting time was calculated from the date of the first, or initial, nomination to the date of the committee hearing. Additionally, when nominees received more than one committee hearing, the statistics used to generate **Figure 3** measure only the length of time from the date a nominee was first nominated to the date of his or her first hearing.

[32] The role of the American Bar Association's Standing Committee on the Federal Judiciary in evaluating judicial candidates may be seen as a factor in the time that a circuit or district court nomination is pending in the Judiciary Committee (but not in the time that a reported nomination is pending on the Senate *Executive Calendar*). If the ABA committee's role is (as it usually has been over the decades) to evaluate judicial candidates before the President selects a nominee, then the ABA's evaluation does not add to the time between when the President makes a nomination and the Senate Judiciary Committee reports it. If, however, the ABA's role is (as it was during the G.W. Bush presidency) to evaluate only after a person has been nominated, then the time taken for that evaluation will add to the total time that the nomination is pending in the Judiciary Committee. A Brookings Institution report noted, however, that the "much longer wait time for Bush's circuit nominees to get hearings ... is explained only partly by the timing of the ABA investigations. (Thirteen Bush nominees got hearings in 2003—after Republicans took control of the Senate; five of those 13 had first been nominated in 2001 or 2002, creating initial-nomination-to-hearing times mostly in the 600 day range)." See Russell Wheeler, "Judicial Nominations and Confirmations after Three Years – Where Do Things Stand," Governance Studies at Brookings, January 13, 2012, p. 7, at http://www.brookings.edu/~/media/research/files/papers/2012/1/13%20nominations%20wheeler/0113_nominations_wheeler.pdf. Note that during the Obama presidency the role of the ABA has reverted back to the practice of evaluating judicial candidates before the President formally selects a nominee.

President Reagan's circuit nominees waited, on average, less time from first nomination to first hearing (28.8 days).

Figure 3. U.S. Circuit and District Court Nominees: Mean and Median Number of Days from Nomination to Hearing for Nominees During First Five Years

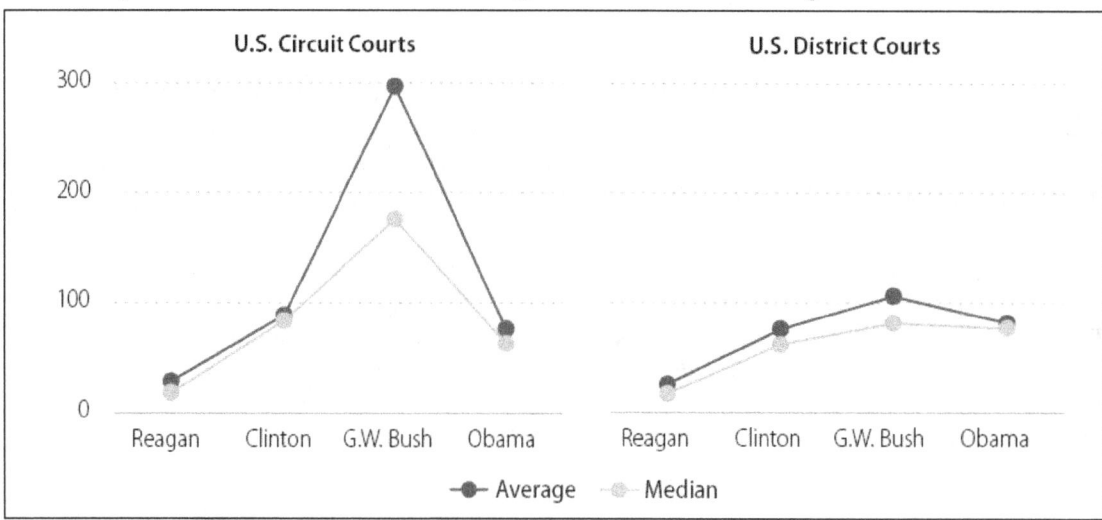

Source: Internal CRS judicial nominations database.

Notes: This figure shows the mean and median number of days from first nomination to first committee hearing for all U.S. circuit and district court nominees who received hearings during a President's first five years in office.

U.S. District Court Nominees

Figure 3 shows, by presidency, less striking differences in the amount of time district court nominees, compared with circuit court nominees, waited for hearings during a President's first five years. The mean and median number of days from first nomination to first hearing for district court nominees ranged from a low of 25.7 and 17.0 days, respectively, during the Reagan presidency to a high of 106.2 and 81.5 days, respectively, during the G.W. Bush presidency.

The average waiting time, from first nomination to first hearing, for President Obama's district court nominees during his first five years, 81.8 days, is close to the average waiting time experienced by district court nominees during the Clinton presidency, 76.1 days. The median number of days for President Obama's and Clinton's district court nominees was 77.0 and 62.0 days, respectively.

Length of Time from Committee Report to Confirmation

A notable change during the Obama presidency has been the length of time judicial nominees await final consideration by the Senate once the Judiciary Committee has finished its work processing a nomination and the nomination has been reported to the full Senate. Specifically, judicial nominations have remained on the *Executive Calendar* for relatively longer periods of time (relative to past President's nominees) before receiving consideration by the full Senate.[33]

---

[33] The calculations on which this statement is based are shown in **Figure 4**. They include days elapsed for nominations (continued...)

Figure 4. U.S. Circuit and District Court Nominees: Mean and Median Number of Days from Committee Report to Confirmation for Nominees Confirmed During First Five Years

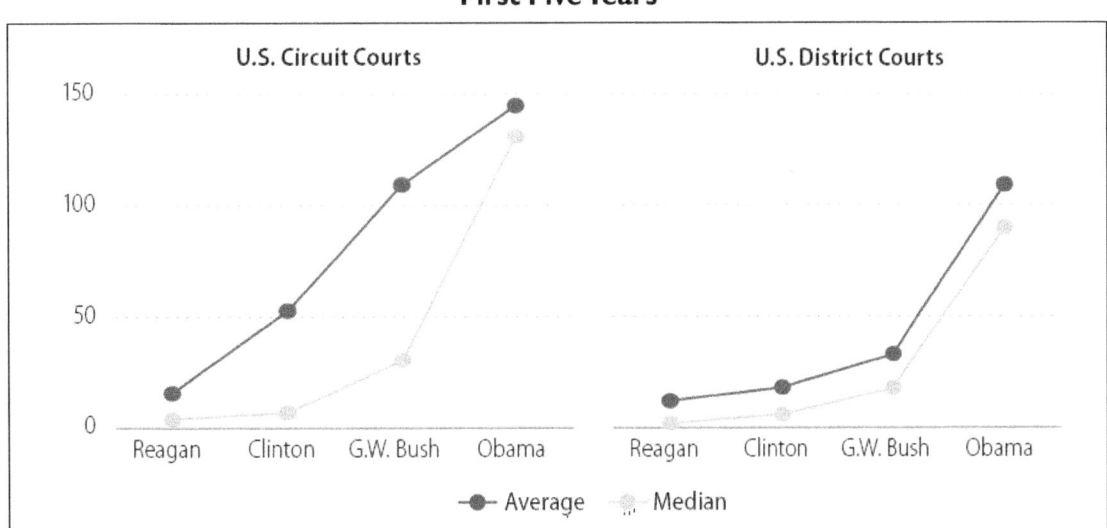

Source: Internal CRS judicial nominations database.

Notes: This figure shows the mean and median number of days from first committee report to confirmation for all U.S. circuit and district court nominees who were confirmed during a President's first five years in office.

U.S. Circuit Court Nominees

For confirmed circuit court nominees during the four presidencies, the fewest days, on average, that elapsed from first committee report to confirmation occurred during the first five years of the Reagan presidency (15.8 days). The mean number of days from committee report to confirmation for nominees who were confirmed during a President's first five years increased to 52.7 days during the first five years of the Clinton presidency and then to 109.4 days during the G.W. Bush presidency. During President Obama's first five years, the average number of days from committee report to confirmation increased to 144.9 days.

The median number of days from first committee report to confirmation ranged from a low of 4 days during the first five years of the Reagan presidency to a high of 131 days during President Obama's first five years. During the first five years of the Clinton and G.W. Bush presidencies, the median number of days from committee report to confirmation were 7 and 30.5 days, respectively.

(...continued)

which were reported out of committee only to be returned to the President, subsequently resubmitted by the President, reported again by the Judiciary Committee, and then confirmed by the Senate. For example, Susan L. Carney was nominated by President Obama to the Second Circuit Court of Appeals. Her nomination was initially reported out of committee on December 1, 2010, during the 111th Congress. Her nomination was returned to the President on December 22, 2010, and resubmitted on January 5, 2011. After being reported by the Judiciary Committee again on February 17, 2011, Ms. Carney's second nomination was confirmed on May 17, 2011, during the 112th Congress. Consequently, the dates used for calculating the number of days between Ms. Carney's nomination being reported out of committee and her confirmation are December 1, 2010, and May 17, 2011.

U.S. District Court Nominees

As with President Reagan's confirmed circuit court nominees, district court nominees during his first five years waited, on average, a shorter amount of time from committee report to confirmation (12.2 days) than did the district nominees confirmed during the first five years of the three other Presidents. The average number of days increased to 18.2 days during the Clinton presidency and to 33.1 days during the G.W. Bush presidency. During the first five years of the Obama presidency, the average number of days increased further to 109.2 days (or approximately 3.5 months).

As **Figure 4** shows, the median number of days from committee report to confirmation ranged from a low of 2.0 days during the Reagan presidency to a high of 90.0 days during the Obama presidency. The median number of days for district nominees confirmed during the first five years of the Clinton and G.W. Bush presidencies were 6.0 and 18.0 days, respectively.

The relatively longer wait times from committee report to confirmation for President Obama's district court nominees did not translate into a majority (or even plurality) of his nominees being broadly opposed, as measured by the number of "nay" votes a nomination received, when confirmed by the Senate.[34]

For example, of the 85 district court nominees whose time from committee report to confirmation was greater than 90.0 days (which is the median identified above for President Obama's district court nominees), 65.0% were confirmed by voice vote or with zero nay votes when a roll call vote was held. Another 14.0% received five or fewer nay votes. Additionally, of the 19 circuit court nominees whose time from nomination to confirmation was greater than 131 days (which is the median for President Obama's circuit court nominees), 10 (52.6%) were confirmed by voice vote or with zero nay votes when a recorded roll call vote was held. Another two (10.5%) were confirmed with fewer than five nay votes.[35]

U.S. Circuit and District Court Vacancies

Percentage of Judgeships Vacant on January 1 of Fifth and Sixth Years in Office

The percentage of vacant circuit and district court judgeships varies over the course of a presidency and is affected, in part, by the pace at which a President selects nominees for vacancies as well as the speed by which the Senate considers the President's nominees.[36] **Table 5**

---

[34] Even if a nominee is largely noncontroversial and receives broad support from the committee, significant delays in filling a judicial vacancy might occur when floor consideration of a judicial nomination on the *Executive Calendar* is delayed or effectively prevented through the use of "holds," or objections to unanimous consent requests. For a discussion of holds in the Senate, generally, see CRS Report 98-712, *"Holds" in the Senate*, by Walter J. Oleszek.

[35] For an analysis of the average and median number of days from committee report to confirmation for circuit and district court nominees during the Clinton, G.W. Bush, and Obama presidencies whose nominations were unopposed on the floor (as well as in committee), see CRS Report R43058, *President Obama's First-Term U.S. Circuit and District Court Nominations: An Analysis and Comparison with Presidents Since Reagan*, by Barry J. McMillion.

[36] The percentage of circuit (or district) court judgeships that are vacant on any given date is calculated by dividing the number of circuit (or district) court vacancies that exist on a date by the number of authorized circuit (or district) court (continued...)

compares for the four Presidents: (i) the percentage of vacant U.S. circuit and district court judgeships on January 1 of a President's fifth year in office; (ii) the percentage of vacant U.S. circuit and district court judgeships vacant on January 1 of a President's sixth year in office; and (iii) the change in the percentage of vacant U.S. circuit and district court judgeships from January 1 of a President fifth's year to January 1 of his sixth year in office.[37]

Table 5. Percentage of U.S. Circuit and District Judgeships Vacant at Beginning of Fifth and Sixth Years in Office

President	Percent of U.S. Circuit Court Judgeships Vacant			Percent of U.S. District Court Judgeships Vacant		
	Jan. 1 of Fifth Year	Jan. 1 of Sixth Year	Change	Jan. 1 of Fifth Year	Jan. 1 of Sixth Year	Change
Reagan	14.9	5.4	-9.5	13.1	7.7	-5.4
Clinton	12.8	12.8	0.0	10.0	9.3	-0.7
G.W. Bush	8.4	7.3	-1.1	3.1	5.2	+2.1
Obama	8.9	9.5	+0.6	8.8	11.1	+2.3

Source: Internal CRS judicial vacancies database; CRS compilation of data provided by the Administrative Office of U.S. Courts.

Notes: This table shows the percentage of U.S. circuit and district court judgeships that were vacant on January 1 of a President's fifth and sixth years in office and the change for the respective type of judgeships between the two dates.

U.S. Circuit Court Vacancies

Table 5 reveals that the percentage of circuit court judgeships that were vacant at the beginning of a President's fifth year in office was greatest during the Reagan and Clinton presidencies (14.9% and 12.8%, respectively) while, at the beginning of a President's sixth year in office, the percentage of circuit court judgeships that were vacant was greatest during the Clinton and Obama presidencies (12.8% and 9.5%, respectively).

Of the four Presidents, President Obama is the only one for whom the percentage of vacant circuit court judgeships increased, albeit slightly, from the beginning of his fifth year to sixth year in office (+0.6%). The percentage of vacant circuit court judgeships declined by 9.5% and 1.1% from the beginning of the fifth to the sixth years of the Reagan and G.W. Bush presidencies, respectively. The percentage of vacant circuit court judgeships on January 1 of President Clinton's sixth year in office was the same as the percentage of such judgeships that were vacant on January 1 of his fifth year in office.

(...continued)

judgeships existing on the same date.

[37] Vacancies data provided by the Administrative Office of U.S. Courts at http://www.uscourts.gov/ JudgesAndJudgeships/JudicialVacancies/ArchiveOfJudicialVacancies.aspx.

U.S. District Court Vacancies

As with circuit court vacancies, the percentage of vacant district court judgeships on January 1 of a President's fifth year in office was greatest during the Reagan and Clinton presidencies (13.1% and 10.0%, respectively). On January 1 of a President's sixth year in office, the percentage of vacant district court judgeships was greatest during the Clinton and Obama presidencies (9.3% and 11.1%, respectively).

From the beginning of a President's fifth to sixth year in office, the percentage of vacant district court judgeships declined during the Reagan presidency (-5.4%) and, slightly, during the Clinton presidency (-0.7%). The percentage of vacant district court judgeships increased from the fifth to sixth years during the G.W. Bush (+2.1%) and Obama (+2.3%) presidencies.[38]

Percentage of Vacancies Deemed Judicial Emergencies on January 1 of Fifth and Sixth Years in Office

A vacancy is deemed a "judicial emergency" by the Judicial Conference by the United States if certain criteria are met regarding the number of case filings for that judgeship or court and, in some cases, the length of time a particular judicial vacancy has existed.[39] As with vacancies, generally, the percentage of vacant circuit and district court judgeships deemed judicial emergencies is affected by a combination of factors. A full accounting is beyond the scope of this report, but such factors include, in part, the pace at which a President selects nominees for vacancies as well as the speed by which the Senate considers the President's nominees.

For circuit court vacancies, a judicial emergency exists if adjusted case filings per appellate panel are in excess of 700 or, for any circuit court vacancy that is in existence for more than 18 months, where adjusted filings are between 500 to 700 per panel. For district court vacancies, a judicial emergency exists when a district court has weighted case filings in excess of 600 per judgeship; or a vacancy is in existence more than 18 months where weighted filings are between 430 to 600 per judgeship; or any district court with more than one authorized judgeship and only one active judge.[40]

Table 6 compares, for President Obama and two of his predecessors, (i) the percentage of circuit and district court vacancies considered judicial emergencies on January 1 of each President's fifth year in office; (ii) the percentage of circuit and district court vacancies considered judicial emergencies on January 1 of each President's sixth year; and (iii) the change in the percentage of judicial vacancies considered judicial emergencies from January 1 of a President's fifth to sixth

---

[38] As reported previously by CRS, President Obama is the only White House occupant since at least President Reagan for whom the district court vacancy rate increased during a presidential first term unaccompanied by the creation of new district court judgeships. See CRS Report R43058, *President Obama's First-Term U.S. Circuit and District Court Nominations: An Analysis and Comparison with Presidents Since Reagan*, by Barry J. McMillion.

[39] The Judicial Conference of the United States is the principal policy making body concerned with the administration of the U.S. courts. The presiding officer of the Judicial Conference is the Chief Justice of the United States and membership of the Conference is comprised of the chief judge of each judicial circuit, the Chief Judge of the Court of International Trade, and a district judge from each regional judicial circuit.

[40] During the Clinton presidency, a judicial emergency was defined as any vacancy in existence for 18 months or longer.

year in office. Data on judicial emergencies is not available for the Reagan presidency; consequently, it is omitted from this part of the analysis.

Table 6. Percentage of Judicial Vacancies Deemed Judicial Emergencies by the Judicial Conference of the United States

President	Percent of U.S. Circuit Court Vacancies			Percent of U.S. District Court Vacancies		
	Jan. 1 of Fifth Year	Jan. 1 of Sixth Year	Change	Jan. 1 of Fifth Year	Jan. 1 of Sixth Year	Change
Clinton[a]	42.1	39.1	-3.0	25.5	33.3	+7.8
G.W. Bush	80.0	61.5	-18.5	28.6	22.9	-5.7
Obama	37.5	58.8	+21.3	35.6	36.0	+0.4

Source: CRS compilation of data provided by the Administrative Office of U.S. Courts.

Notes: This table shows the percentage of judicial vacancies deemed judicial emergencies by the Judicial Conference of the United States on January 1 of a President's fifth and sixth years in office and the change for the respective type of judgeships between the two dates.

a.   The percentages reported for January 1 of President Clinton's fifth year in office (i.e., January 1, 1997) are based on data for December 1, 1996. Data related to judicial emergencies existing on January 1, 1997 are not available.

U.S. Circuit Court Vacancies

Table 6 reveals that the percentage of vacant circuit court judgeships considered judicial emergencies on January 1 of a President's fifth year in office was greatest during the G.W. Bush presidency (80.0%), followed by the Clinton and Obama presidencies (42.1% and 37.5%, respectively). The percentage of such vacancies considered judicial emergencies on January 1 of a President's sixth year in office was also greatest during the G.W. Bush presidency (61.5%). The percentage of circuit court vacancies considered judicial emergencies at the beginning of President Obama's and Clinton's sixth years was 58.8% and 39.1%, respectively.

Of the three Presidents, President Obama is the only one for whom the percentage of vacant circuit court judgeships deemed judicial emergencies increased from January 1 of his fifth year to January 1 of his sixth year (increasing from 37.5% to 58.8%). For Presidents G.W. Bush and Clinton the percentage of vacant circuit court judgeships considered judicial emergencies decreased by 18.5% and 3.0%, respectively.

U.S. District Court Vacancies

As shown by **Table 6**, the percentage of vacant district court judgeships considered judicial emergencies on January 1 of a President's fifth year in office was greatest during the Obama presidency (35.6%), followed by the G.W. Bush and Clinton presidencies (28.6% and 25.5%, respectively). The percentage of such vacancies considered judicial emergencies on January 1 of a President's sixth year in office was also greatest during the Obama presidency (36.0%). The percentage of district court vacancies considered judicial emergencies at the beginning of President G.W. Bush's and Clinton's sixth years was 22.9% and 33.3%, respectively.

President G.W. Bush is the only one of the three Presidents for whom the percentage of vacant district court judgeships deemed judicial emergencies declined from January 1 of his fifth to sixth year in office (i.e., declining from 28.6% to 22.9%). For Presidents Clinton and Obama the percentage of vacant circuit court judgeships considered judicial emergencies increased (by 7.8% and 0.4%, respectively) from January 1 of each President's fifth to sixth year.

Author Contact Information

Barry J. McMillion
Analyst on the Federal Judiciary
bmcmillion@crs.loc.gov, 7-6025

www.ingramcontent.com/pod-product-compliance
Lightning Source LLC
Chambersburg PA
CBHW080809290526
45790CB00008B/3627